Introduction

Definition of 5G Technology:

5G, short for the fifth generation of mobile networks, represents a significant leap forward in wireless communication technology. Unlike its predecessors, 5G is designed to connect virtually everyone and everything, including machines, objects, and devices. It promises to deliver higher speeds, lower latency, and increased capacity, enabling a new era of connectivity and innovation. Imagine being able to download a full-length HD movie in seconds or having a seamless, lag-free virtual reality experience – these are just glimpses of what 5G technology can offer.

Explanation of 5G as the Fifth Generation of Mobile Networks:

As the fifth generation of mobile networks, 5G builds upon the foundation laid by previous generations. Each generation has brought new capabilities and improvements, and 5G is no exception. It aims to address the growing demand for data and connectivity, driven by the proliferation of smartphones, IoT devices, and emerging technologies. With its enhanced performance and capabilities, 5G is set to revolutionize various industries and transform the way we live, work, and communicate.

Key Features: Higher Speeds, Lower Latency, Increased Capacity:

One of the most notable features of 5G is its significantly higher speeds. While 4G networks offer peak download speeds of around 1 Gbps, 5G can deliver speeds of up to 10 Gbps or more, depending on the implementation. This increase in speed enables faster data transfer, smoother streaming, and more responsive applications.

Another critical feature of 5G is its ultra-low latency. Latency refers to the time it takes for data to travel from one point to another. In 4G networks, latency typically ranges from 30 to 50 milliseconds. However, 5G aims to reduce this to as low as 1 millisecond, making real-time communication and applications, such as autonomous vehicles and remote surgery, more feasible and reliable.

Increased capacity is another key advantage of 5G. As more devices connect to the internet, existing networks face congestion and slower speeds. 5G addresses this issue by efficiently utilizing the available spectrum and employing advanced technologies like Massive MIMO (Multiple Input Multiple Output) and beamforming. This increased capacity ensures that more devices can be connected simultaneously without compromising performance.

Historical Context: Evolution from 1G to 4G:

To fully appreciate the significance of 5G, it is essential to understand the evolution of mobile networks from 1G to 4G. The journey began with 1G, the first generation of wireless cellular technology, introduced in the 1980s. 1G networks were analog and primarily focused on voice communication. They provided basic mobile phone services with limited coverage and quality.

The introduction of 2G in the early 1990s marked the transition from analog to digital communication. 2G networks offered improved voice quality, enhanced security, and support for text messaging (SMS). This generation laid the groundwork for mobile data services, although speeds were still relatively slow.

The arrival of 3G in the early 2000s brought significant advancements in mobile data capabilities. 3G networks enabled faster internet access, video calling, and mobile applications. Users could browse the web, send emails, and stream media on their mobile devices, although speeds were still limited compared to today's standards.

4G, introduced in the late 2000s, revolutionized mobile communication by providing high-speed internet access and supporting a wide range of data-intensive applications. With peak speeds reaching up to 1 Gbps, 4G networks enabled seamless streaming, online gaming, and video conferencing. The widespread adoption of smartphones and the proliferation of mobile apps further fueled the demand for faster and more reliable connectivity.

Brief History of Mobile Networks:

The history of mobile networks is a story of continuous innovation and technological advancement. Each generation has built upon the successes and shortcomings of its predecessor, driving the evolution of wireless communication. From the basic voice services of 1G to the high-speed data capabilities of 4G, mobile networks have transformed our lives and reshaped industries.

Key milestones in this journey include the transition from analog to digital with 2G, the introduction of mobile data services with 3G, and the high-speed internet access provided by 4G. These advancements have paved the way for the next generation, 5G, which promises to take connectivity to new heights and unlock a wealth of opportunities.

Understanding 5G Technology

Technical Specifications of 5G

Frequency Spectrum (Low-band, Mid-band, High-band):

5G technology operates across three primary frequency bands: low-band, mid-band, and high-band. Each band has distinct characteristics and plays a crucial role in the overall performance of 5G networks.

- Low-band (below 1 GHz): This frequency range provides wide coverage and good penetration through obstacles like buildings and trees. However, it offers lower data speeds compared to higher frequency bands. Low-band 5G is ideal for rural and suburban areas where extensive coverage is essential.

- Mid-band (1 GHz to 6 GHz): Mid-band frequencies strike a balance between coverage, speed, and capacity. They offer faster data rates than low-band frequencies while maintaining a reasonable coverage area. This makes mid-band 5G suitable for urban and suburban environments, providing a good mix of speed and coverage.

- High-band (above 24 GHz): Also known as millimeter wave (mmWave) frequencies, high-band 5G offers extremely high data speeds and capacity. However, the coverage area is limited, and the signal struggles to penetrate obstacles. High-band 5G is best suited for dense urban areas, stadiums, and other high-traffic locations where speed and capacity are paramount.

Latency and Speed Improvements:

One of the most significant advancements in 5G technology is its ability to drastically reduce latency and increase data speeds. Latency refers to the time it takes for data to travel from the source to the destination and back. In 4G networks, latency typically ranges from 30 to 50 milliseconds. 5G aims to reduce this to as low as 1 millisecond, enabling real-time communication and applications.

The speed improvements with 5G are equally impressive. While 4G networks offer peak download speeds of up to 1 Gbps, 5G can achieve speeds of up to 10 Gbps or more. This means that users can download large files, stream high-definition videos, and engage in data-intensive activities with minimal delay.

Network Slicing and Edge Computing:

Network slicing is a revolutionary feature of 5G that allows operators to create multiple virtual networks within a single physical 5G network. Each slice can be tailored to meet specific requirements, such as bandwidth, latency, and reliability. This enables service providers to offer customized solutions for different industries and applications, such as autonomous vehicles, smart cities, and industrial automation.

Edge computing is another critical component of 5G technology. It involves processing data closer to the source, at the edge of the network, rather than in a centralized data center. This reduces latency and improves the performance of applications that require real-time processing, such as augmented reality

(AR), virtual reality (VR), and IoT devices. By bringing computing resources closer to the user, 5G enables faster and more efficient data processing.

Comparison with Previous Generations (1G to 4G)

Evolution of Mobile Networks: From Analog Voice Calls to High-Speed Data:

The journey of mobile networks began with 1G, the first generation of wireless cellular technology, introduced in the 1980s. 1G networks were analog and primarily focused on voice communication, providing basic mobile phone services with limited coverage and quality.

The introduction of 2G in the early 1990s marked the transition from analog to digital communication. 2G networks offered improved voice quality, enhanced security, and support for text messaging (SMS). This generation laid the groundwork for mobile data services, although speeds were still relatively slow.

3G, introduced in the early 2000s, brought significant advancements in mobile data capabilities. 3G networks enabled faster internet access, video calling, and mobile applications. Users could browse the web, send emails, and stream media on their mobile devices, although speeds were still limited compared to today's standards.

The arrival of 4G in the late 2000s revolutionized mobile communication by providing high-speed internet access and supporting a wide range of data-intensive applications. With peak speeds reaching up to 1 Gbps, 4G networks enabled seamless streaming, online gaming, and video conferencing. The widespread adoption of smartphones and the proliferation of mobile apps further fueled the demand for faster and more reliable connectivity.

Key Differences and Improvements in 5G

5G technology brings several key improvements over previous generations:

- Speed: 5G offers peak download speeds of up to 10 Gbps, compared to 1 Gbps in 4G.

- Latency: 5G aims to reduce latency to as low as 1 millisecond, compared to 30-50 milliseconds in 4G.

- Capacity: 5G can support up to 1 million devices per square kilometer, significantly more than 4G.

- Reliability: 5G provides ultra-reliable low latency communications (URLLC) for critical applications.

- Flexibility: Network slicing allows for customized virtual networks to meet specific requirements.

Key Enablers of 5G Technology

Massive MIMO (Multiple Input Multiple Output):

Massive MIMO is a technology that enhances the capacity and coverage of 5G networks by using multiple antennas at both the transmitter and receiver ends. Traditional MIMO systems use a few antennas, but massive MIMO can employ hundreds of antennas simultaneously. This increases the amount of data that can be transmitted and received, improving network performance and efficiency.

By directing multiple data streams to multiple users simultaneously, massive MIMO increases spectral efficiency and supports a higher number of connected devices. This is particularly important in densely populated areas where network congestion is a concern.

Beamforming:

Beamforming is a technique that directs wireless signals to specific users rather than broadcasting them in all directions. By using advanced algorithms and antenna arrays, beamforming focuses the signal toward the intended recipient, reducing interference and increasing the signal strength.

This targeted approach enhances the overall performance of the network, providing better coverage and higher data rates, especially in challenging environments with many obstacles. Beamforming is a critical component of 5G, enabling more efficient use of the available spectrum and improving user experience.

Small Cells and Infrastructure Changes:

To support the high data rates and low latency of 5G, network infrastructure needs to be densified with small cells. Small cells are low-powered radio access nodes that cover a smaller area than traditional macro cells. They can be deployed on street lights, utility poles, buildings, and other structures, providing enhanced coverage and capacity in high-traffic areas.

The deployment of small cells helps to alleviate network congestion and ensures consistent performance in densely populated urban areas. This densification of networks is essential for realizing the full potential of 5G technology, enabling faster data speeds and lower latency.

5G technology is poised to revolutionize wireless communication with its higher speeds, lower latency, and increased capacity. By leveraging advanced techniques like massive MIMO, beamforming, and network slicing, 5G offers unprecedented performance and flexibility. As we move forward, the deployment of small cells and edge computing will further enhance the capabilities of 5G, paving the way for a new era of connectivity and innovation.

5G Network Architecture

Core Network vs. Radio Access Network (RAN):

The architecture of 5G networks is divided into two primary components: the Core Network and the Radio Access Network (RAN). Each plays a crucial role in ensuring the seamless operation of the 5G network.

Core Network:

The Core Network is the central part of the 5G network responsible for handling data transfer, internet connectivity, and network management. It acts as the backbone of the entire system, connecting the RAN to external networks like the internet and other mobile networks. Key functions of the Core Network include:

- Data Routing: Directing data packets between the user devices and external networks.

- Session Management: Establishing and maintaining communication sessions between devices.

- Subscriber Management: Handling user authentication, billing, and mobility management.

- Network Slicing: Creating virtual networks tailored to specific services or industries, each with its own performance characteristics.

The 5G Core Network, often referred to as the 5GC, is designed to support the diverse range of services that 5G offers, from high-speed mobile broadband to ultra-reliable low latency communications.

Radio Access Network (RAN):

The Radio Access Network (RAN) is the part of the 5G network that connects user devices to the Core Network. It comprises base stations, antennas, and other infrastructure that enable wireless communication. The RAN handles the following functions:

- Signal Transmission and Reception: Sending and receiving radio signals to and from user devices.

- Resource Management: Allocating radio spectrum resources to ensure efficient communication.

- Mobility Management: Managing handovers and maintaining connectivity as users move between cells.

The RAN is divided into different types of cells, including macrocells, microcells, and small cells, each serving different coverage areas and capacities. Small cells, in particular, are crucial for 5G, providing enhanced coverage and capacity in densely populated urban areas.

Standalone (SA) vs. Non-Standalone (NSA) Architectures:

5G networks can be deployed in two main architectures: Standalone (SA) and Non-Standalone (NSA). Each has its advantages and deployment scenarios.

Standalone (SA) Architecture

In Standalone (SA) architecture, the 5G network operates independently of existing 4G infrastructure. It uses a 5G Core Network (5GC) and 5G RAN, providing a complete end-to-end 5G experience. The SA architecture offers several benefits:

- Full 5G Capabilities: Enables all 5G features, including network slicing, ultra-low latency, and enhanced mobile broadband.

- Future-Proof: Designed to support future advancements and services that 5G can offer.

- Enhanced Performance: Provides better performance, lower latency, and higher efficiency compared to NSA.

However, deploying SA architecture requires significant investment in new infrastructure, which may delay widespread adoption.

Non-Standalone (NSA) Architecture:

Non-Standalone (NSA) architecture leverages existing 4G infrastructure to deliver 5G services. In this model, the 5G RAN is used in conjunction with the existing 4G Core Network (EPC). This approach allows for a quicker and more cost-effective deployment of 5G services. Key characteristics of NSA architecture include:

- Leveraging Existing Infrastructure: Utilizes existing 4G networks to roll out 5G services rapidly.

- Incremental Upgrades: Allows operators to gradually transition to 5G without immediate large-scale infrastructure investments.

- Improved User Experience: Provides enhanced speeds and capacity by combining 4G and 5G resources.

While NSA architecture enables a faster rollout, it does not support the full range of 5G capabilities, such as network slicing and ultra-low latency, which are only available in the SA architecture.

Role of Software-Defined Networking (SDN) and Network Functions Virtualization (NFV)

Software-Defined Networking (SDN):

Software-Defined Networking (SDN) is a network management approach that separates the control plane from the data plane. This separation allows network administrators to manage network services through software, leading to more flexible and efficient network operations. In the context of 5G, SDN offers several advantages:

- Network Agility: Enables dynamic adjustments to network configurations in response to changing traffic patterns and service requirements.

- Centralized Control: Provides a centralized view of the network, simplifying management and reducing operational complexity.

- Cost Efficiency: Reduces the need for specialized hardware, leading to cost savings.

Network Functions Virtualization (NFV):

Network Functions Virtualization (NFV) is a technology that virtualizes network functions, allowing them to run on standard commercial off-the-shelf (COTS) hardware instead of proprietary hardware appliances. NFV enhances 5G networks by:

- Flexibility: Enables the deployment of network functions on demand, adapting to varying network conditions and service requirements.

- Scalability: Allows for the easy scaling of network resources to handle increased traffic or new services.

- Reduced Costs: Lowers capital and operational expenses by using standardized hardware and reducing reliance on proprietary equipment.

Together, SDN and NFV play a critical role in the 5G network architecture, enabling greater flexibility, efficiency, and cost-effectiveness. They allow network operators to quickly deploy new services, adapt to changing demands, and optimize network performance.

Security Considerations and Challenges in 5G Networks

Key Security Concerns:

As 5G networks become more complex and interconnected, they face several security challenges. Key concerns include:

- Increased Attack Surface: The proliferation of connected devices and the use of various frequency bands increase the potential entry points for cyberattacks.

- Privacy Issues: The vast amount of data generated by 5G networks raises concerns about data privacy and protection.

- Supply Chain Risks: The reliance on multiple vendors for 5G infrastructure components can introduce vulnerabilities if any part of the supply chain is compromised.

- Network Slicing Vulnerabilities: While network slicing offers numerous benefits, it also presents new security challenges, as each slice may have different security requirements and exposures.

Potential Solutions

To address these security concerns, several measures can be implemented:

- Enhanced Encryption: Using advanced encryption techniques to protect data in transit and at rest.

- Robust Authentication: Implementing strong authentication mechanisms to ensure that only authorized devices and users can access the network.

- Security by Design: Incorporating security measures into the design and development of 5G infrastructure and devices from the outset.

- Continuous Monitoring: Employing advanced monitoring and anomaly detection systems to identify and respond to potential threats in real-time.

- Collaboration and Standards: Working with industry stakeholders, regulatory bodies, and standardization organizations to develop and enforce robust security standards for 5G networks.

The 5G network architecture, with its core and radio access components, standalone and non-standalone deployment models, and the incorporation of SDN and NFV, represents a significant advancement in wireless communication technology. While it brings numerous benefits in terms of speed, latency, and capacity, it also introduces new security challenges that must be addressed to ensure the safe and reliable operation of 5G networks. By understanding these components and addressing the associated challenges, we can fully leverage the transformative potential of 5G technology.

The Impact of 5G on Connectivity

Enhanced Mobile Broadband (eMBB):

Enhanced Mobile Broadband (eMBB) is one of the primary use cases of 5G technology, aimed at significantly improving data speeds and overall user experiences. With eMBB, users can expect peak download speeds of up to 10 Gbps, which is a substantial increase compared to the 1 Gbps peak speeds offered by 4G networks. This leap in speed enables a wide range of data-intensive applications and services that were previously impractical or impossible.

For example, with eMBB, users can download high-definition movies in seconds, participate in high-quality video conferencing without lag, and stream 4K or even 8K videos with minimal buffering. This enhanced capability is particularly beneficial in urban areas with high population densities, where network congestion has traditionally led to slower speeds and reduced performance.

Moreover, eMBB supports the growing demand for mobile data driven by the proliferation of smartphones, tablets, and other connected devices. As more people rely on mobile internet for work, education, and entertainment, the enhanced capacity and speed of eMBB ensure a smooth and seamless user experience, even in crowded environments.

Ultra-Reliable Low Latency Communications (URLLC):

Ultra-Reliable Low Latency Communications (URLLC) is another critical aspect of 5G technology, designed to support applications that require real-time responses and high reliability. With latency as low as 1 millisecond, URLLC enables a new class of applications that were previously unattainable with older network generations.

One of the most prominent applications of URLLC is in autonomous vehicles. Self-driving cars need to communicate with each other and with traffic infrastructure in real-time to make split-second decisions and ensure safety. The ultra-low latency of 5G makes this possible, enabling vehicles to respond to changing conditions almost instantaneously.

Similarly, URLLC plays a vital role in remote surgery and telemedicine. Surgeons can perform operations on patients located thousands of miles away with the help of robotic instruments controlled over 5G networks. The low latency ensures that the surgeon's movements are accurately mirrored by the robotic instruments in real-time, reducing the risk of errors and improving patient outcomes.

Other applications of URLLC include industrial automation, where real-time control of machinery and processes is essential, and gaming, where low latency is crucial for a smooth and immersive experience.

Massive Machine-Type Communications (mMTC):

Massive Machine-Type Communications (mMTC) refers to the ability of 5G networks to connect a vast number of IoT devices simultaneously. With mMTC, 5G can support up to 1 million devices per square kilometer, which is a significant increase compared to previous generations.

This capability is essential for the widespread adoption of IoT technologies across various industries. In smart cities, for example, mMTC enables the deployment of a multitude of sensors and devices to monitor and manage everything from traffic flow and air quality to energy consumption and waste management. The interconnectedness of these devices allows for more efficient and sustainable urban living.

In agriculture, mMTC supports smart farming techniques by connecting numerous sensors and devices that monitor soil conditions, crop health, and weather patterns. This data-driven approach enables farmers to make more informed decisions, optimize resource use, and increase crop yields.

The healthcare sector also benefits from mMTC, with the ability to connect wearable devices, remote monitoring systems, and other medical equipment. This connectivity allows for continuous monitoring of patients' health conditions, timely interventions, and improved overall care.

Impact on Mobile Users and Consumer Experiences:

The impact of 5G on mobile users and consumer experiences is profound, transforming the way we interact with technology and access information.

Streaming Services: Higher Quality and Lower Buffering:

One of the most noticeable improvements with 5G is in streaming services. The higher data speeds and increased capacity of 5G networks mean that users can enjoy higher quality video and audio streaming with virtually no buffering. Whether watching movies, TV shows, or live events, 5G ensures a smooth and uninterrupted experience, even in high-demand situations like major sports events or concerts.

Augmented Reality (AR) and Virtual Reality (VR): Immersive Experiences:

5G also opens up new possibilities for augmented reality (AR) and virtual reality (VR) applications. The low latency and high bandwidth of 5G networks enable more immersive and interactive AR and VR experiences. For example, users can explore virtual environments, participate in virtual meetings, or engage in interactive gaming without the lag or disconnections that can disrupt the experience.

In retail, AR can enhance the shopping experience by allowing customers to virtually try on clothes or see how furniture would look in their homes. In education, VR can provide immersive learning experiences, such as virtual field trips or hands-on training in simulated environments.

Gaming and Entertainment: Reduced Latency and Improved Performance:

The gaming industry is set to benefit significantly from 5G technology. Reduced latency is crucial for online gaming, where even a slight delay can impact gameplay and user experience. With 5G, gamers can enjoy smoother, more responsive gameplay, whether playing on mobile devices or using cloud-based gaming services.

Additionally, 5G enables new forms of interactive entertainment, such as live multiplayer VR games and location-based AR games that require real-time data processing and low-latency communication. These advancements create more engaging and dynamic gaming experiences that were not possible with previous network generations.

5G technology brings significant improvements in mobile broadband, ultra-reliable low latency communications, and massive machine-type communications. These advancements enhance connectivity, support a wide range of applications, and transform consumer experiences in streaming, AR/VR, gaming, and more. As 5G networks continue to roll out globally, the full potential of these technologies will become increasingly evident, driving innovation and shaping the future of connectivity.

5G and the Internet of Things (IoT)

Definition and Scope of IoT:

The Internet of Things (IoT) refers to the network of physical devices, vehicles, appliances, and other objects embedded with sensors, software, and connectivity, enabling them to collect and exchange data. The IoT ecosystem includes a wide range of devices, from simple sensors to complex machinery, all interconnected to create a seamless flow of information.

The scope of IoT is vast, encompassing various sectors and applications. It includes smart homes with interconnected appliances, industrial automation systems, health monitoring devices, and smart city infrastructure. By integrating these devices into a cohesive network, IoT enables real-time data collection, analysis, and decision-making, leading to increased efficiency, productivity, and innovation.

Explanation of IoT and Its Applications:

IoT applications span across numerous industries, each leveraging the technology to address specific needs and challenges:

- Smart Homes: IoT enables homeowners to control lighting, heating, security systems, and appliances remotely through connected devices. For instance, smart thermostats can adjust temperature settings based on user preferences and occupancy, optimizing energy consumption.

- Healthcare: IoT devices like wearable health monitors, smartwatches, and remote patient monitoring systems collect real-time health data, allowing healthcare providers to monitor patients' conditions, detect anomalies, and provide timely interventions.

- Industrial Automation: In manufacturing, IoT connects machinery, sensors, and control systems to monitor and optimize production processes, predict maintenance needs, and reduce downtime.

- Agriculture: IoT in agriculture, or smart farming, uses sensors and connected devices to monitor soil conditions, weather patterns, and crop health, enabling precision agriculture techniques that improve yield and resource efficiency.

- Transportation: IoT enhances vehicle-to-everything (V2X) communication, connecting vehicles to each other, traffic infrastructure, and central management systems to improve traffic flow, reduce accidents, and support autonomous driving.

How 5G Enhances IoT Capabilities:

5G technology significantly enhances IoT capabilities by addressing key limitations of previous network generations. Its advanced features enable the deployment of more robust, efficient, and scalable IoT solutions.

Connectivity Density:

One of the primary enhancements of 5G is its ability to support a much higher density of connected devices. While 4G networks can connect around 100,000 devices per square kilometer, 5G can support up to 1 million devices in the same area. This increased connectivity density is crucial for environments like smart cities and industrial settings, where numerous devices need to operate simultaneously without network congestion.

Power Efficiency:

5G technology improves power efficiency, which is critical for battery-operated IoT devices. Low-power wide-area (LPWA) technologies integrated into 5G, such as NB-IoT (Narrowband IoT) and LTE-M (Long-Term Evolution for Machines), enable devices to operate on minimal power for extended periods. This results in longer battery life and reduces the need for frequent recharging or replacement, making IoT deployments more sustainable and cost-effective.

Reliability and Latency Improvements:

The ultra-reliable low latency communications (URLLC) feature of 5G ensures high reliability and minimal latency, which are essential for time-sensitive IoT applications. With latency as low as 1 millisecond, 5G supports real-time data transmission and processing, making it suitable for critical applications like autonomous driving, remote surgery, and industrial automation.

Applications of 5G in IoT

Smart Cities: Intelligent Infrastructure and Services:

5G-powered IoT enables the development of smart cities, where various urban systems and services are interconnected and managed efficiently. Smart city applications include:

- Smart Lighting: Streetlights equipped with sensors can adjust brightness based on the time of day and pedestrian presence, reducing energy consumption and improving safety.

- Waste Management: IoT-enabled waste bins can signal when they need to be emptied, optimizing collection routes and reducing operational costs.

- Traffic Management: Connected traffic lights and sensors can monitor traffic flow and adjust signals in real-time to reduce congestion and improve traffic efficiency.

Industrial IoT (IIoT): Automation and Efficiency in Manufacturing:

In the industrial sector, 5G enhances IoT applications by providing reliable, high-speed connectivity for machinery and control systems. Key applications include:

- Predictive Maintenance: Sensors on machinery can monitor performance and predict potential failures, allowing for timely maintenance and reducing downtime.

- Automation: 5G supports the automation of production lines, enabling real-time communication between robots, sensors, and control systems for efficient and precise manufacturing processes.

- Supply Chain Management: IoT devices can track the movement and condition of goods throughout the supply chain, ensuring transparency, reducing losses, and improving inventory management.

Healthcare and Remote Monitoring: Improved Patient Care:

5G-enabled IoT transforms healthcare by facilitating remote patient monitoring, telemedicine, and smart medical devices. Applications include:

- Remote Patient Monitoring: Wearable devices and sensors can continuously monitor patients' vital signs and transmit data to healthcare providers, allowing for proactive health management and timely interventions.

- Telemedicine: High-speed 5G connectivity supports real-time video consultations and remote diagnostics, making healthcare more accessible, especially in rural and underserved areas.

- Smart Medical Devices: IoT-enabled medical devices, such as insulin pumps and heart monitors, can automatically adjust treatment based on real-time data, improving patient outcomes and reducing the need for manual intervention.

Agriculture and Smart Farming: Precision Agriculture Techniques:

5G technology enhances smart farming by providing reliable connectivity for a wide range of agricultural IoT devices. Key applications include:

- Soil and Crop Monitoring: Sensors in the fields can monitor soil moisture, nutrient levels, and crop health, providing farmers with data to optimize irrigation, fertilization, and pest control.

- Weather Stations: Connected weather stations provide real-time weather data, helping farmers make informed decisions about planting, harvesting, and protecting crops from adverse weather conditions.

- Livestock Management: IoT devices can monitor the health and location of livestock, improving animal welfare and productivity.

Autonomous Vehicles and Transportation: Enhanced Vehicle-to-Everything (V2X) Communication:

5G plays a crucial role in the development and deployment of autonomous vehicles and intelligent transportation systems. Applications include:

- Vehicle-to-Vehicle (V2V) Communication: Autonomous vehicles can communicate with each other to share information about road conditions, traffic, and potential hazards, enhancing safety and coordination.

- Vehicle-to-Infrastructure (V2I) Communication: Vehicles can interact with traffic lights, road signs, and other infrastructure to receive real-time updates and optimize routes.

- Vehicle-to-Pedestrian (V2P) Communication: Connected vehicles can detect and communicate with pedestrians and cyclists, reducing accidents and improving road safety.

5G significantly enhances the capabilities of IoT by providing high connectivity density, improved power efficiency, and ultra-reliable low latency communications. These advancements enable a wide range of applications across various sectors, including smart cities, industrial automation, healthcare, agriculture, and transportation. As 5G networks continue to expand, the transformative potential of IoT will become increasingly evident, driving innovation and improving the quality of life.

Transforming Global Communication

Impact on International Communication and Collaboration:

The advent of 5G technology is revolutionizing international communication and collaboration by providing unprecedented levels of connectivity and data transmission speeds. The enhanced capabilities of 5G networks facilitate seamless communication across borders, enabling businesses, governments, and individuals to interact more effectively and efficiently.

One of the most significant impacts of 5G on global communication is the ability to conduct real-time video conferencing and collaborative work without latency issues. This is particularly important in the context of global business operations, where teams spread across different continents can collaborate on projects as if they were in the same room. The increased bandwidth and lower latency of 5G ensure high-quality video and audio, making remote meetings more productive and engaging.

Additionally, 5G technology supports the widespread adoption of cloud services, enabling organizations to store and access data from anywhere in the world. This capability enhances global cooperation, as employees can access the same resources and applications regardless of their geographical location. For example, multinational companies can streamline their operations and improve efficiency by leveraging cloud-based platforms for project management, data analysis, and customer relationship management.

Moreover, 5G is driving the development of new communication tools and platforms that leverage augmented reality (AR) and virtual reality (VR). These immersive technologies enable more interactive and engaging communication experiences, from virtual trade shows and conferences to remote training and education programs. By breaking down geographical barriers, 5G fosters a more interconnected and collaborative global community.

5G in Developing Countries: Opportunities and Challenges:

The deployment of 5G technology in developing countries presents both significant opportunities and challenges. On the one hand, 5G has the potential to drive economic growth, improve access to education and healthcare, and enhance the quality of life for millions of people. On the other hand, the rollout of 5G infrastructure in these regions faces numerous hurdles that must be addressed.

Opportunities:

1. Economic Growth: 5G can stimulate economic development by enabling new business models and industries, such as telemedicine, smart agriculture, and e-commerce. Enhanced connectivity can attract foreign investment and create new job opportunities, boosting local economies.

2. Access to Education: 5G technology can bridge educational gaps by providing remote

learning opportunities to students in underserved areas. High-speed internet access enables the delivery of interactive and engaging educational content, allowing students to participate in virtual classrooms and access online resources.

3. Healthcare Improvements: Telemedicine and remote healthcare services can be significantly enhanced with 5G, providing patients in remote or rural areas with access to medical expertise and care. This can lead to better health outcomes and reduced healthcare disparities.

4. Infrastructure Development: The deployment of 5G networks can drive the development of critical infrastructure, such as power grids and transportation systems, by enabling smart grid technologies and intelligent transportation systems.

Challenges:

1. High Costs: The deployment of 5G infrastructure requires substantial investment in new base stations, fiber optic cables, and

other equipment. Developing countries may struggle to secure the necessary funding, which could delay the rollout of 5G networks.

2. Regulatory Hurdles: Complex regulatory environments and bureaucratic processes can impede the deployment of 5G networks. Governments in developing countries need to streamline regulations and provide incentives for private sector investment in 5G infrastructure.

3. Technical Expertise: The successful deployment and maintenance of 5G networks require specialized technical skills and expertise. Developing countries may face a shortage of skilled professionals, which could hinder the implementation and operation of 5G networks.

4. Digital Divide: While 5G has the potential to bridge the digital divide, there is a risk that it could exacerbate existing inequalities if not deployed equitably. Efforts must be made to ensure that underserved and remote areas are prioritized in the rollout of 5G networks.

Role of 5G in Bridging the Digital Divide:

5G technology has the potential to play a crucial role in bridging the digital divide by providing high-speed internet access to underserved and remote areas. By connecting these regions to the global digital economy, 5G can help reduce inequalities and promote inclusive growth.

In many developing countries, rural and remote areas lack reliable internet access, limiting opportunities for education, healthcare, and economic development. 5G's ability to provide high-speed connectivity with low latency can address these challenges by enabling the deployment of wireless broadband services in areas where laying fiber optic cables is impractical or cost-prohibitive.

For instance, 5G-powered fixed wireless access (FWA) can deliver high-speed internet to homes and businesses in remote areas, providing a viable alternative to traditional wired connections. This can support remote education, telemedicine, and small businesses, fostering economic and social development in these communities.

Moreover, 5G can enable the deployment of IoT devices and applications that address specific challenges faced by rural communities. For example, smart agriculture solutions can help farmers optimize their use of resources, improve crop yields, and reduce environmental impact. Similarly, remote health monitoring systems can provide real-time data to healthcare providers, enabling timely interventions and improving patient outcomes.

To ensure that 5G contributes to bridging the digital divide, it is essential for governments, private sector stakeholders, and international organizations to collaborate on initiatives that promote equitable access to 5G technology. This includes investing in infrastructure, providing affordable connectivity solutions, and implementing policies that support digital inclusion.

Case Studies: Global Deployment and Usage Scenarios

South Korea: Leading the 5G Revolution:

South Korea is one of the first countries to roll out nationwide 5G networks, setting a benchmark for other nations. The country has seen significant adoption of 5G technology across various sectors, including manufacturing, healthcare, and entertainment.

- Smart Factories: South Korea has implemented 5G-enabled smart factories that leverage IoT, AI, and automation to enhance production efficiency and quality. These factories use real-time data to monitor and optimize manufacturing processes, reducing downtime and operational costs.

- Healthcare Innovations: South Korean hospitals are using 5G to enable remote consultations and real-time monitoring of patients. For example, 5G-powered telemedicine platforms allow doctors to conduct virtual consultations with patients in remote areas, providing timely medical care and reducing the need for travel.

- Entertainment and Media: The entertainment industry in South Korea is leveraging 5G to offer immersive experiences, such as live streaming concerts and sports events in virtual reality. This has transformed the way audiences engage with content, providing new opportunities for content creators and broadcasters.

China: Expanding 5G Coverage:

China has made significant strides in deploying 5G networks, with a focus on expanding coverage and driving innovation across various industries.

- Smart Cities: Several Chinese cities have implemented 5G-powered smart city solutions, including intelligent traffic management, smart lighting, and public safety systems. These solutions use real-time data to improve urban planning, reduce traffic congestion, and enhance the quality of life for residents.

- Agriculture: In rural China, 5G is being used to support precision agriculture techniques. Farmers are using IoT sensors to monitor soil conditions, weather patterns, and crop health, enabling data-driven decision-making and improving agricultural productivity.

- Autonomous Vehicles: China is at the forefront of autonomous vehicle development, with 5G playing a crucial role in enabling vehicle-to-everything (V2X) communication. This technology allows autonomous vehicles to communicate with each other and with traffic infrastructure, improving safety and efficiency on the roads.

United States: Driving Innovation:

The United States has been a key player in the development and deployment of 5G technology, with a focus on innovation and commercialization.

- Industrial IoT: American companies are leveraging 5G to enhance industrial IoT applications, such as predictive maintenance and automated production lines. For example, manufacturers are using 5G-connected sensors to monitor equipment performance and predict maintenance needs, reducing downtime and improving efficiency.

- Telemedicine: The COVID-19 pandemic has accelerated the adoption of telemedicine in the United States, with 5G enabling high-quality video consultations and remote patient monitoring. This has improved access to healthcare services, particularly for patients in rural and underserved areas.

- Public Safety: 5G is being used to enhance public safety and emergency response services. First responders can use 5G-connected devices to access real-time information, coordinate responses, and communicate more effectively during emergencies.

The deployment of 5G technology is transforming global communication, enhancing connectivity, and fostering international collaboration. By addressing the challenges of deploying 5G in developing countries and leveraging its potential to bridge the digital divide, we can create a more inclusive and connected world. The case studies from South Korea, China, and the United States demonstrate the diverse applications and benefits of 5G, highlighting its transformative impact across various sectors. As 5G networks continue to expand, the global community will witness unprecedented advancements in communication, collaboration, and innovation.

Economic and Social Implications

Economic Benefits of 5G

Job Creation and New Industries:

The rollout of 5G technology is poised to be a significant driver of economic growth, primarily through the creation of new jobs and industries. The deployment of 5G infrastructure requires a skilled workforce, leading to an increase in jobs related to network installation, maintenance, and management. Additionally, the development and manufacturing of 5G-enabled devices, such as smartphones, IoT gadgets, and smart home appliances, further contribute to job creation in the tech sector.

Beyond direct employment, 5G fosters the emergence of new industries and business models. For instance, the enhanced connectivity and low latency of 5G support the growth of autonomous vehicles, smart manufacturing, and telehealth services. These industries not only create new jobs but also stimulate innovation and entrepreneurship, driving economic diversification and resilience.

Increased Productivity and Efficiency:

5G technology significantly boosts productivity and efficiency across various sectors. In manufacturing, 5G-enabled industrial IoT (IIoT) systems allow for real-time monitoring and control of production processes, reducing downtime and optimizing resource use. Predictive maintenance, powered by 5G, helps manufacturers anticipate equipment failures and schedule timely repairs, further enhancing operational efficiency.

In the logistics and supply chain industry, 5G enables precise tracking of goods, real-time inventory management, and automated warehousing solutions. These advancements streamline operations, reduce costs, and improve delivery times, benefiting businesses and consumers alike.

The agricultural sector also benefits from 5G through smart farming techniques. IoT sensors connected via 5G provide farmers with detailed data on soil conditions, crop health, and weather patterns, enabling precision agriculture practices that increase yield and reduce waste.

Social Impact

Education and Remote Learning:

One of the most profound social impacts of 5G is in the realm of education. The high-speed, low-latency connectivity provided by 5G supports remote learning and virtual classrooms, making education more accessible to students regardless of their geographical location. During the COVID-19 pandemic, the need for reliable remote education solutions became evident, and 5G technology plays a crucial role in ensuring that students can participate in online classes, access digital resources, and engage with interactive learning tools.

For instance, 5G enables virtual reality (VR) and augmented reality (AR) applications in education, providing immersive learning experiences that can enhance understanding and retention of complex subjects. Students can explore historical sites, conduct virtual science experiments, or participate in interactive simulations, all from the comfort of their homes.

Healthcare Access and Telemedicine:

5G technology is revolutionizing healthcare by enhancing telemedicine and remote patient monitoring. The high-speed connectivity and low latency of 5G allow for real-time video consultations, enabling patients to receive medical advice and treatment from healthcare providers without the need to travel. This is particularly beneficial for individuals in rural and underserved areas, where access to healthcare facilities may be limited.

Remote patient monitoring systems, powered by 5G, enable continuous tracking of patients' vital signs and health conditions. Wearable devices and smart sensors collect real-time data, which is transmitted to healthcare providers for analysis. This allows for timely interventions and better management of chronic conditions, improving patient outcomes and reducing healthcare costs.

5G also supports the use of advanced medical technologies, such as robotic surgery and AI-driven diagnostics. Surgeons can perform complex procedures remotely using robotic instruments, guided by real-time data transmitted over 5G networks. AI algorithms can analyze medical images and data with high accuracy, assisting doctors in diagnosing and treating diseases more effectively.

Impact on Rural and Underserved Areas:

One of the key promises of 5G is its potential to bridge the digital divide and improve connectivity in rural and underserved areas. Traditional wired broadband infrastructure is often expensive and challenging to deploy in these regions, leaving many communities without reliable internet access. 5G, with its ability to provide high-speed wireless connectivity, offers a viable solution to this problem.

Fixed wireless access (FWA) using 5G technology can deliver broadband internet to homes and businesses in remote areas, enabling them to access online services, participate in e-commerce, and connect with the global digital economy. This can lead to economic development, job creation, and improved quality of life in these communities.

Enhanced connectivity also supports various social services in rural areas, such as telehealth, online education, and e-government services. By providing reliable internet access, 5G empowers individuals and communities to access essential services, reducing disparities and promoting social inclusion.

Regulatory and Policy Considerations

Spectrum Allocation and Management:

The successful deployment of 5G networks requires careful management of the radio frequency spectrum, which is a limited and valuable resource. Governments and regulatory bodies play a crucial role in allocating and managing spectrum to ensure that it is used efficiently and equitably.

Spectrum allocation involves assigning specific frequency bands for 5G use, balancing the needs of mobile network operators, public safety agencies, and other spectrum users. Regulators must also ensure that spectrum is allocated in a way that promotes competition and innovation, preventing monopolistic practices and encouraging investment in new technologies.

In addition to allocation, effective spectrum management includes monitoring and enforcing compliance with spectrum usage regulations, mitigating interference between different users, and facilitating spectrum sharing where appropriate. This requires collaboration between regulatory bodies, industry stakeholders, and international organizations to develop harmonized standards and best practices.

Privacy and Data Protection:

The widespread adoption of 5G technology and the proliferation of connected devices raise important privacy and data protection concerns. As more personal and sensitive data is transmitted and processed over 5G networks, it is essential to ensure that this data is adequately protected from unauthorized access, breaches, and misuse.

Regulatory frameworks and policies must be in place to safeguard user privacy and data security. This includes implementing robust encryption standards, enforcing strict data protection regulations, and ensuring transparency in how data is collected, stored, and used. Companies and service providers must also adopt best practices for cybersecurity, including regular audits, vulnerability assessments, and incident response plans.

Furthermore, international cooperation is necessary to address cross-border data flows and ensure that data protection standards are upheld globally. As 5G networks facilitate global communication and data exchange, harmonizing privacy regulations and fostering collaboration between countries become increasingly important.

5G technology brings significant economic and social benefits, including job creation, increased productivity, improved access to education and healthcare, and enhanced connectivity in rural and underserved areas. However, the successful realization of these benefits requires careful consideration of regulatory and policy issues, such as spectrum allocation and data protection. By addressing these challenges and fostering an inclusive and secure 5G ecosystem, we can unlock the full potential of 5G technology and drive sustainable development and social progress.

Beyond 5G: Future Wireless Technologies

Introduction to 6G and Its Potential:

As 5G networks continue to be deployed and adopted worldwide, the next generation of wireless technology, known as 6G, is already on the horizon. 6G promises to build on the advancements of 5G, delivering even greater speed, lower latency, and more sophisticated connectivity solutions. While 5G has set the stage for a connected world, 6G aims to create a more intelligent, immersive, and integrated digital environment.

Expected Advancements and Timelines:

6G is expected to bring several key advancements over 5G, including:

- Higher Data Rates: 6G aims to achieve data rates of up to 1 Tbps, significantly surpassing the peak speeds of 5G. This will enable instantaneous data transfer and support more data-intensive applications.

- Ultra-Low Latency: Building on the low latency of 5G, 6G targets latency as low as 100 microseconds, facilitating real-time interactions and applications.

- Enhanced Connectivity: 6G will support even higher device densities, accommodating the growing number of IoT devices and enabling more extensive machine-to-machine communication.

- Intelligent Networks: 6G networks will leverage advanced artificial intelligence (AI) and machine learning (ML) algorithms to optimize performance, manage resources, and enhance security autonomously.

The development and standardization of 6G technology are anticipated to progress throughout the 2020s, with initial commercial deployments expected around 2030. Research institutions, technology companies, and governments are already investing in 6G research and development to ensure a smooth transition from 5G and to unlock the full potential of this next-generation technology.

Potential Use Cases and Applications:

The potential applications of 6G are vast and varied, encompassing numerous industries and aspects of daily life. Some of the most promising use cases include:

- Holographic Communication: 6G could enable high-fidelity holographic displays for communication, allowing users to interact with lifelike 3D images in real time. This could revolutionize remote meetings, entertainment, and virtual collaboration.

- Extended Reality (XR): While 5G supports augmented reality (AR) and virtual reality (VR), 6G will take these experiences to the next level with more immersive, responsive, and seamless extended reality (XR) applications, blending the physical and digital worlds.

- Digital Twins: 6G can facilitate the creation of highly detailed and dynamic digital twins of physical objects, systems, and environments. These digital replicas can be used for real-time monitoring, simulation, and optimization in industries such as manufacturing, healthcare, and urban planning.

- Advanced Robotics: 6G's ultra-low latency and high reliability will enable the deployment of advanced robotics for applications like remote surgery, autonomous industrial operations, and precision agriculture.

- Global Connectivity: 6G aims to provide ubiquitous connectivity, ensuring that even the most remote and underserved areas have access to high-speed internet and digital services, further bridging the digital divide.

Emerging Technologies in Wireless Communication

Terahertz Communication:

Terahertz (THz) communication refers to the use of electromagnetic waves in the terahertz frequency range (0.1-10 THz) for wireless data transmission. Terahertz waves offer several advantages, including extremely high data rates and large bandwidth, making them ideal for future wireless communication systems.

- High Data Rates: Terahertz communication can achieve data rates in the range of terabits per second (Tbps), supporting ultra-fast data transfer and enabling applications like real-time holographic communication and high-resolution video streaming.

- Short Range: Due to their short wavelength, terahertz waves have a limited range and are susceptible to atmospheric absorption. However, they are well-suited for short-range, high-capacity applications such as indoor wireless networks, data centers, and wireless backhaul links.

Research in terahertz communication focuses on developing efficient terahertz transceivers, improving signal propagation, and addressing challenges related to range and atmospheric absorption.

Visible Light Communication (VLC):

Visible Light Communication (VLC) is a wireless communication technology that uses visible light to transmit data. VLC systems use LED lights to modulate data signals, which are then detected by photodiodes or cameras.

- High Data Rates: VLC can achieve high data rates by utilizing the wide bandwidth of visible light. This makes it suitable for applications requiring fast and reliable data transfer.

- Energy Efficiency: VLC systems can leverage existing lighting infrastructure, such as LED bulbs, to provide both illumination and data communication, reducing energy consumption and infrastructure costs.

- Security: Visible light signals do not penetrate walls, offering a higher level of security compared to traditional radio frequency (RF) communication. This makes VLC suitable for secure communication in environments like offices, hospitals, and government buildings.

VLC research focuses on improving modulation techniques, developing efficient photodetectors, and integrating VLC with existing communication systems to create hybrid networks.

Research and Development Trends

Ongoing Projects and Future Prospects:

The development of 6G and other future wireless technologies is driven by a wide range of research and development initiatives undertaken by academic institutions, technology companies, and government agencies worldwide. Key trends and areas of focus include:

- AI and ML Integration: Researchers are exploring ways to integrate AI and ML into wireless networks to enhance performance, optimize resource allocation, and improve security. AI-driven networks can adapt to changing conditions in real time, providing more efficient and reliable communication.

- Advanced Modulation and Coding: Developing new modulation and coding schemes is essential for achieving higher data rates and improving spectral efficiency. Researchers are investigating techniques like orbital angular momentum (OAM) modulation and advanced error correction codes.

- Spectrum Utilization: Efficient use of the spectrum is critical for future wireless communication. Research efforts are focused on spectrum sharing, dynamic spectrum access, and the use of higher frequency bands, such as terahertz and millimeter waves.

- Energy Efficiency: As the number of connected devices grows, energy efficiency becomes increasingly important. Researchers are working on energy-efficient communication protocols, low-power hardware, and techniques to reduce the energy consumption of wireless networks.

- Security and Privacy: Ensuring the security and privacy of wireless communication is a top priority. Ongoing research aims to develop robust encryption methods, secure communication protocols, and techniques to detect and mitigate cyber threats.

The future of wireless communication lies in the development and deployment of 6G and other emerging technologies like terahertz communication and visible light communication. These advancements promise to deliver unprecedented data rates, ultra-low latency, and intelligent network management, enabling a wide range of innovative applications and transforming industries and everyday life. As research and development continue to progress, the vision of a fully connected, intelligent, and immersive digital world is becoming increasingly attainable.

Challenges and Risks

Technical Challenges in Deploying 5G

Infrastructure Costs and Deployment Hurdles:

One of the most significant challenges in deploying 5G networks is the substantial cost associated with the necessary infrastructure. Unlike previous generations, 5G requires a denser network of base stations and small cells to ensure adequate coverage and capacity. This densification is essential for achieving the high data rates and low latency that 5G promises, but it also drives up costs considerably.

The deployment process itself involves numerous hurdles, including the installation of new hardware, the upgrading of existing infrastructure, and the integration of advanced technologies like Massive MIMO and beamforming. These tasks demand significant financial investment and technical expertise, posing a challenge for network operators, especially in less developed regions where resources and skilled labor may be limited.

Moreover, obtaining the necessary permits and approvals from local authorities can be a time-consuming and complex process. Regulatory frameworks vary widely across different countries and even within regions of the same country, complicating the deployment process. Navigating these bureaucratic landscapes adds further delays and costs to the rollout of 5G networks.

Interference and Spectrum Management:

Effective spectrum management is crucial for the successful deployment of 5G networks. The use of higher frequency bands, such as millimeter waves (mmWave), presents unique challenges in terms of interference and signal propagation. Higher frequencies are more susceptible to physical obstructions, such as buildings and trees, and have shorter transmission ranges compared to lower frequency bands.

Managing interference between different spectrum users, including existing services like satellite communication and radar systems, is another critical issue. Ensuring that 5G networks can coexist with these services without causing harmful interference requires careful planning and coordination.

Dynamic spectrum sharing and advanced interference mitigation techniques are essential to address these challenges. However, implementing these solutions adds complexity to network design and operation, requiring continuous monitoring and optimization to maintain network performance and reliability.

Security Risks and Vulnerabilities

Cybersecurity Threats:

The increased connectivity and complexity of 5G networks introduce new cybersecurity risks and vulnerabilities. As more devices and critical infrastructure are connected to 5G networks, the potential attack surface for cyber threats expands significantly. Cybersecurity threats in the 5G era include data breaches, denial-of-service (DoS) attacks, and the exploitation of vulnerabilities in network components and connected devices.

The integration of IoT devices, many of which have limited security features, exacerbates these risks. Compromised IoT devices can be used as entry points for cybercriminals to infiltrate networks, launch attacks, or steal sensitive data. Additionally, the use of software-defined networking (SDN) and network functions virtualization (NFV) in 5G networks introduces new vectors for cyberattacks, as these technologies rely heavily on software and virtualization.

Mitigation Strategies and Best Practices:

To mitigate cybersecurity risks in 5G networks, several strategies and best practices should be implemented:

- Robust Encryption: Employing strong encryption methods to protect data in transit and at rest is essential. This ensures that even if data is intercepted, it cannot be easily deciphered and misused.

- Multi-Factor Authentication (MFA): Implementing MFA for network access helps verify the identities of users and devices, reducing the risk of unauthorized access.

- Regular Security Audits: Conducting regular security audits and vulnerability assessments helps identify and address potential weaknesses in the network infrastructure and connected devices.

- Network Segmentation: Segregating different parts of the network helps contain potential breaches and limits the spread of attacks. This is particularly important for critical infrastructure and sensitive data.

- AI and ML for Threat Detection: Leveraging AI and ML technologies for real-time threat detection and response can enhance network security. These technologies can analyze vast amounts of data to identify anomalies and potential threats more quickly and accurately than traditional methods.

- Collaboration and Information Sharing: Collaborating with industry stakeholders, government agencies, and cybersecurity organizations to share information about emerging threats and best practices is crucial for staying ahead of cybercriminals.

Health and Environmental Concerns

Studies on 5G Radiation and Health Impacts:

The deployment of 5G networks has raised concerns about the potential health effects of increased exposure to radiofrequency (RF) radiation. While the frequencies used in 5G networks are higher than those used in previous generations, they still fall within the non-ionizing portion of the electromagnetic spectrum, which means they do not have enough energy to ionize atoms or molecules.

Numerous studies have been conducted to assess the health impacts of RF radiation, including those specific to 5G frequencies. The consensus among health authorities, such as the World Health Organization (WHO) and the International Commission on Non-Ionizing Radiation Protection (ICNIRP), is that the RF exposure levels associated with 5G networks are within safe limits and do not pose a significant health risk.

However, public concerns persist, and ongoing research is essential to monitor any potential long-term health effects. Transparent communication and adherence to established safety standards are critical in addressing these concerns and building public trust.

Environmental Sustainability:

The environmental impact of 5G networks is another important consideration. The deployment and operation of 5G infrastructure require significant energy consumption, contributing to the overall carbon footprint of the telecommunications industry. Additionally, the manufacturing and disposal of network equipment and devices can have environmental implications.

To mitigate these impacts, several strategies can be employed:

- Energy-Efficient Technologies: Developing and deploying energy-efficient network equipment and technologies can help reduce the energy consumption of 5G networks. This includes using advanced cooling systems, energy-saving protocols, and renewable energy sources.

- Recycling and E-Waste Management: Implementing robust recycling programs and responsible e-waste management practices can minimize the environmental impact of disposing of old network equipment and devices. Encouraging the reuse and refurbishment of devices can also extend their lifecycle and reduce waste.

- Sustainable Deployment Practices: Adopting sustainable practices during the deployment of 5G infrastructure, such as minimizing land use and environmental disruption, can help mitigate the impact on local ecosystems.

While the deployment of 5G networks brings numerous benefits, it also presents several challenges and risks that must be addressed. The high costs and complexity of infrastructure deployment, cybersecurity threats, and potential health and environmental concerns require careful planning and management. By implementing effective strategies and best practices, stakeholders can overcome these challenges and ensure the successful and sustainable deployment of 5G technology.

Case Studies and Real-World Applications

Detailed Case Studies of 5G Implementation

Smart Cities

Singapore:

Singapore has positioned itself as a global leader in smart city initiatives, leveraging 5G technology to enhance urban living. The city-state's Smart Nation initiative aims to harness technology to improve the quality of life for its residents, create more economic opportunities, and build a more inclusive society.

- Smart Infrastructure: Singapore uses 5G-enabled sensors and IoT devices to monitor and manage public utilities such as water supply, electricity, and waste management. This real-time data collection and analysis help optimize resource usage and improve efficiency.

- Public Safety: The deployment of 5G technology supports high-definition surveillance cameras and drones for real-time monitoring and quick response to emergencies. These systems enhance public safety and security by providing better situational awareness and coordination among emergency services.

- Transportation: Singapore's transport network benefits from 5G through smart traffic management systems that use real-time data to reduce congestion and improve traffic flow. Autonomous vehicles are also being tested, with 5G providing the necessary low-latency communication for safe and efficient operation.

Barcelona:

Barcelona is another example of a city utilizing 5G to become smarter and more connected. The city's efforts focus on improving public services, enhancing sustainability, and fostering innovation.

- Smart Lighting: Barcelona uses 5G-connected smart streetlights that adjust brightness based on the time of day and pedestrian activity, reducing energy consumption and improving public safety.

- Environmental Monitoring: 5G-enabled sensors monitor air quality, noise levels, and weather conditions in real-time. This data helps the city implement measures to improve environmental quality and public health.

- Citizen Engagement: The city has developed mobile applications that provide residents with real-time information on public services, transportation, and community events. These apps use 5G connectivity to offer a seamless user experience and encourage greater civic participation.

Industrial Applications

Factories:

In the manufacturing sector, 5G technology is transforming factories into highly efficient, automated production environments. One notable example is Bosch's smart factory in Stuttgart, Germany.

- Predictive Maintenance: Bosch uses 5G-connected sensors to monitor the condition of machinery in real-time. Data analytics and AI predict potential failures, allowing for timely maintenance and reducing downtime.

- Robotics and Automation: The factory employs 5G-powered robots and automated guided vehicles (AGVs) for various tasks, such as assembly, material handling, and quality inspection. The low latency of 5G ensures precise and coordinated movements, enhancing productivity and safety.

- Data-Driven Decision Making: Real-time data from the production floor is integrated into a central management system, providing insights that help optimize processes, reduce waste, and improve product quality.

Ports:

Ports are also benefiting from 5G technology, enhancing their operations and efficiency. The Port of Rotterdam in the Netherlands is a prime example.

- Smart Logistics: The port uses 5G to connect various logistics processes, including cargo tracking, automated cranes, and autonomous vehicles. This connectivity ensures smooth and efficient cargo handling, reducing delays and costs.

- Remote Operations: 5G enables remote control and monitoring of equipment, such as cranes and tugboats, from centralized control centers. This enhances operational safety and allows for better resource management.

- Environmental Impact: The port employs 5G-connected sensors to monitor environmental conditions, such as water quality and emissions. This data helps the port implement sustainable practices and comply with environmental regulations.

Healthcare Innovations

Remote Surgeries:

5G technology is revolutionizing healthcare by enabling remote surgeries and improving patient outcomes. A notable example is the collaboration between Vodafone and the Italian Institute of Technology (IIT) for remote surgical procedures.

- Real-Time Data Transmission: 5G's ultra-low latency allows surgeons to perform complex procedures remotely with robotic instruments. Real-time data transmission ensures that the surgeon's movements are accurately mirrored by the robotic instruments, reducing the risk of errors.

- Enhanced Imaging: High-definition imaging systems powered by 5G provide surgeons with detailed views of the surgical site, improving precision and outcomes. This technology is particularly useful for minimally invasive surgeries.

- Access to Specialists: Remote surgeries enable patients in underserved or remote areas to access specialist care without the need to travel. This can significantly improve healthcare access and outcomes for patients with limited options.

Transportation

Autonomous Vehicles:

Autonomous vehicles (AVs) rely heavily on 5G technology for safe and efficient operation.

One leading example is the deployment of AVs in Silicon Valley, California, by companies like Waymo and Tesla.

- Vehicle-to-Vehicle (V2V) Communication: AVs use 5G to communicate with each other, sharing information about their positions, speeds, and intended maneuvers. This communication helps prevent collisions and improves traffic flow.

- Vehicle-to-Infrastructure (V2I) Communication: 5G allows AVs to interact with traffic signals, road signs, and other infrastructure elements. This enables optimized routing, adaptive traffic management, and enhanced safety.

- Real-Time Data Processing: The low latency and high bandwidth of 5G support real-time processing of data from sensors and cameras on AVs. This enables rapid decision-making and precise control, ensuring safe navigation in complex environments.

Smart Highways:

Smart highways are another transportation application benefiting from 5G technology. The A2/M2 connected corridor in the United Kingdom is a notable example.

- Connected Road Infrastructure: The corridor uses 5G-connected sensors and communication systems to monitor traffic conditions, weather, and road surface quality. This data is used to provide real-time information to drivers and optimize traffic management.

- Enhanced Safety: Smart highways can detect accidents, hazards, and congestion, providing timely alerts to drivers and emergency services. This improves road safety and reduces response times.

- Autonomous Vehicle Integration: The corridor is designed to support autonomous vehicles, with 5G enabling seamless communication between AVs and road infrastructure. This facilitates the safe and efficient integration of AVs into existing traffic.

Lessons Learned and Best Practices

Key Takeaways from Successful
Implementations:

- Collaborative Partnerships: Successful 5G
implementations often involve collaboration
between multiple stakeholders, including
government agencies, technology companies,
and industry partners. These partnerships
help align objectives, share expertise, and
pool resources.

- Regulatory Support: Supportive regulatory
frameworks are crucial for the timely and
efficient deployment of 5G networks.
Governments can facilitate this by
streamlining approval processes, allocating
spectrum, and providing incentives for
investment.

- Public Awareness and Engagement:
Educating the public about the benefits and
safety of 5G technology is essential for
gaining acceptance and support. Transparent
communication and addressing public
concerns can help build trust and foster a
positive perception of 5G.

- Scalability and Flexibility: Designing 5G
networks with scalability and flexibility in mind

ensures that they can adapt to future demands and technological advancements. Modular infrastructure and software-defined networking are key enablers of this flexibility.

- Focus on Security: Implementing robust cybersecurity measures from the outset is critical to protecting 5G networks and connected devices. Regular security assessments, encryption, and multi-factor authentication are essential components of a comprehensive security strategy.

- Sustainability Considerations: Incorporating sustainability into 5G deployment plans can help minimize environmental impact and promote long-term viability. Energy-efficient technologies, recycling programs, and sustainable deployment practices are important elements of this approach.

Real-world applications of 5G technology in smart cities, industrial settings, healthcare, and transportation demonstrate its transformative potential. By learning from successful implementations and adopting best practices, stakeholders can maximize the benefits of 5G and address the challenges associated with its deployment. This will pave the way for a more connected, efficient, and innovative future.

Glossary of Terms

- 5G: The fifth generation of mobile network technology, offering higher speeds, lower latency, and increased capacity compared to previous generations.

- 6G: The future sixth generation of mobile network technology, expected to offer even greater advancements in speed, latency, and connectivity.

- Augmented Reality (AR): A technology that overlays digital information and images onto the physical world, enhancing the user's perception of their environment.

- Beamforming: A signal processing technique used in 5G networks to direct wireless signals toward specific devices, improving signal strength and quality.

- Core Network: The central part of a telecommunications network that provides various services and manages data and voice traffic.

- Cybersecurity: The practice of protecting systems, networks, and data from digital attacks, unauthorized access, and damage.

- Edge Computing: A computing paradigm that processes data closer to the data source or end-user to reduce latency and improve performance.

- Enhanced Mobile Broadband (eMBB): A key use case of 5G technology that provides higher data speeds and improved user experiences for mobile broadband services.

- Fixed Wireless Access (FWA): A method of providing internet access using wireless technology instead of traditional wired connections, often used in rural or underserved areas.

- Holographic Communication: A communication technology that uses holograms to create lifelike 3D images for remote interactions.

- Internet of Things (IoT): A network of interconnected devices that collect and exchange data, enabling automation and real-time monitoring across various applications.

- Latency: The time it takes for data to travel from the source to the destination and back, measured in milliseconds (ms).

- Massive MIMO (Multiple Input Multiple Output): A technology that uses multiple antennas at both the transmitter and receiver ends to increase capacity and coverage in wireless networks.

- Millimeter Wave (mmWave): A high-frequency band (30 GHz to 300 GHz) used in 5G networks to provide high data rates over short distances.

- Network Functions Virtualization (NFV): A technology that virtualizes network functions, allowing them to run on standard hardware instead of specialized equipment.

- Network Slicing: A technique that divides a physical network into multiple virtual networks, each optimized for different types of services or applications.

- Non-Standalone (NSA) Architecture: A 5G deployment model that leverages existing 4G infrastructure to provide 5G services.

- Radio Access Network (RAN): The part of a telecommunications network that connects user devices to the core network.

- Software-Defined Networking (SDN): A network management approach that separates the control plane from the data plane, allowing for centralized network control and optimization.

- Standalone (SA) Architecture: A 5G deployment model that uses a dedicated 5G core network and radio access network, providing a full 5G experience.

- Telemedicine: The use of telecommunications technology to provide remote medical care and consultations.

- Ultra-Reliable Low Latency Communications (URLLC): A key use case of 5G technology that provides high reliability and low latency for applications requiring real-time responses.

- Visible Light Communication (VLC): A wireless communication technology that uses visible light to transmit data.

List of Key Standards and Regulatory Bodies

Organizations and Standards Relevant to 5G and Wireless Communication:

- 3rd Generation Partnership Project (3GPP): A global collaboration of telecommunications standards organizations that develop protocols for mobile networks, including 5G.

- International Telecommunication Union (ITU): A specialized agency of the United Nations responsible for coordinating global telecommunications standards and spectrum management.

- Federal Communications Commission (FCC): The U.S. regulatory body responsible for managing and regulating communications by radio, television, wire, satellite, and cable.

- European Telecommunications Standards Institute (ETSI): An independent, nonprofit organization that produces globally applicable standards for information and communications technologies, including 5G.

- International Electrotechnical Commission (IEC): An international standards organization that prepares and publishes standards for electrical, electronic, and related technologies.

- Institute of Electrical and Electronics Engineers (IEEE): A professional association that develops global standards in a broad range of industries, including telecommunications.

- Global System for Mobile Communications Association (GSMA): An industry organization that represents the interests of mobile network operators worldwide and promotes the development of mobile communication standards.

- National Institute of Standards and Technology (NIST): A U.S. agency that develops and promotes measurement standards, including those related to cybersecurity and wireless communication.

- International Commission on Non-Ionizing Radiation Protection (ICNIRP): An independent scientific organization that provides guidance and recommendations on the health and environmental effects of non-ionizing radiation, including RF radiation from wireless technologies.

These organizations and standards play a crucial role in the development, deployment, and regulation of 5G and future wireless technologies, ensuring that they are safe, efficient, and widely accessible.

www.ingramcontent.com/pod-product-compliance
Lightning Source LLC
Chambersburg PA
CBHW070848070326
40690CB00009B/1749